HOW DOES IT WORK?: FARM TECH
MILKERS

by Johannah Luza

T0020118

pogo

Ideas for Parents and Teachers

Pogo Books let children practice reading informational text while introducing them to nonfiction features such as headings, labels, sidebars, maps, and diagrams, as well as a table of contents, glossary, and index.

Carefully leveled text with a strong photo match offers early fluent readers the support they need to succeed.

Before Reading

- "Walk" through the book and point out the various nonfiction features. Ask the student what purpose each feature serves.
- Look at the glossary together. Read and discuss the words.

Read the Book

- Have the child read the book independently.
- Invite him or her to list questions that arise from reading.

After Reading

- Discuss the child's questions. Talk about how he or she might find answers to those questions.
- Prompt the child to think more. Ask: Modern milking machines run on engines. Can you name other machines that run on engines?

Pogo Books are published by Jump!
5357 Penn Avenue South
Minneapolis, MN 55419
www.jumplibrary.com

Library of Congress Cataloging-in-Publication Data is available at www.loc.gov or upon request from the publisher.

ISBN: 979-8-88524-691-0 (hardcover)
ISBN: 979-8-88524-692-7 (paperback)
ISBN: 979-8-88524-693-4 (ebook)

Editor: Eliza Leahy
Designer: Emma Almgren-Bersie
Content Consultant: Santosh K. Pitla, Ph.D., Biological Systems Engineering

Photo Credits: yod 67/Shutterstock, cover; M Kunz/Shutterstock, 1; Hurst Photo/Shutterstock, 3; Prostock-studio/Shutterstock, 4; andresr/iStock, 5; Vereshchagin Dmitry/Shutterstock, 6; World History Archive/Alamy, 7; PixHound/iStock, 8-9; Alexander Zamaraev/Shutterstock, 10-11; Vladimir Mulder/Shutterstock, 12-13; Wayne HUTCHINSON/Alamy, 14-15; Chris6/iStock, 16; Tim Scrivener/Alamy, 17; SeventyFour/iStock, 18-19; GAUTIER Stephane/SAGAPHOTO.COM/Alamy, 20-21; stefan11/Shutterstock, 23.

Printed in the United States of America at Corporate Graphics in North Mankato, Minnesota.

TABLE OF CONTENTS

CHAPTER 1

DAIRY COWS

What goes great with cookies? A glass of milk! But have you ever thought about where milk comes from? There are many kinds of milk. Much of the milk humans drink comes from dairy cows.

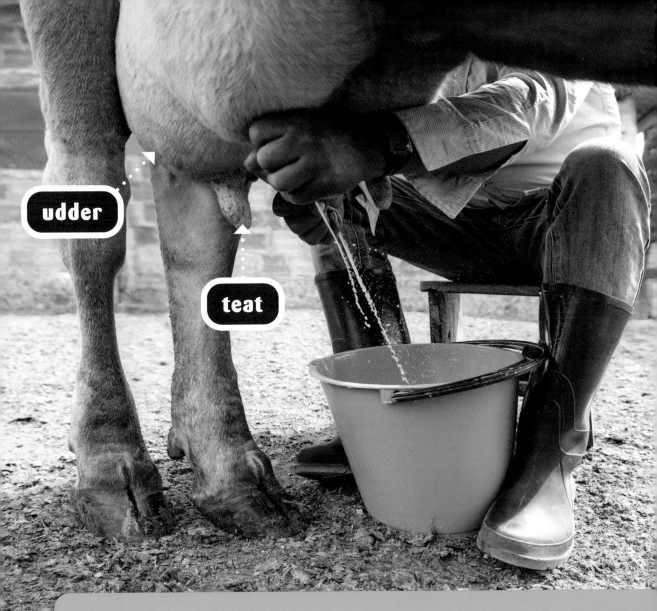

udder

teat

People have been milking cows for more than 9,000 years! For most of this time, people milked cows by hand. A female cow's udder holds milk. The udder has four teats. A teat is squeezed. Milk comes out!

CHAPTER 2

MILKERS AT WORK

Today, machines help milk cows. We call them milkers. The first milker was invented in 1878 by Anna Baldwin. Milkers made milking cows more **efficient**.

milker

Early milkers had hand pumps. Using **suction**, the machines pulled on cows' teats continuously. This caused the cows discomfort.

hand pump

Surge Bucket Milker

Early milkers were hard to clean. Because of this, **bacteria** spread to the cows' teats. Sometimes this caused **infections**. It also made the milk unsafe to drink.

In 1922, the Surge Bucket Milker was invented. It was easy to clean. There were only four pieces of rubber to wash. More farmers started using it. Many farmers still use this kind of milker.

DID YOU KNOW?

It takes one hour to milk six cows by hand. In the same amount of time, a milker can milk 100 cows!

Over time, milkers became simpler to use. This made the process quicker. How? Instead of hand pumps, modern milkers run on **engines**. This gives farmers more time to do other tasks.

TAKE A LOOK!

What are the parts of a modern milker, and how does it work? Take a look!

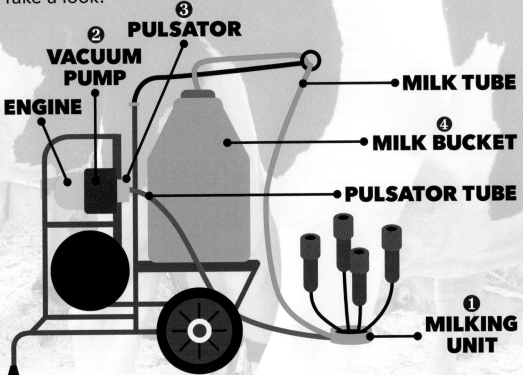

② VACUUM PUMP
③ PULSATOR
ENGINE
MILK TUBE
④ MILK BUCKET
PULSATOR TUBE
① MILKING UNIT

❶ The milking unit attaches to a cow's teats.
❷ A **vacuum** uses suction to remove the milk.
❸ The pulsator moves like the sucking pattern of a **calf** drinking milk from its mother.
❹ Milk comes out of the cow's teats. It goes through a tube to the milk bucket.

rotary parlor

Today, farmers often use milking parlors. These are buildings in which many cows go to be milked at the same time. One kind is like a merry-go-round for cows! It is called a rotary parlor.

Cows are **herded** into the rotary parlor. The platform slowly spins. As it spins, a farmer attaches a milker to each cow. When the milking is complete, the farmer removes the milkers.

platform

CHAPTER 3

ROBOTIC MILKERS

With new technology, the farmer doesn't have to be part of milking. A cow enters a stall. A camera finds the teats. The machine washes and dries them. Then, a **robotic** arm connects the milker to the teats.

robotic arm

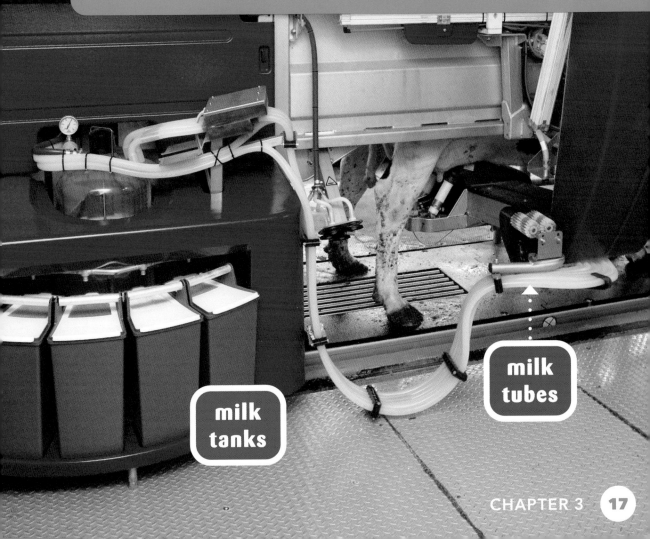

An **automatic milking system (AMS)** milks a cow in about seven minutes. During milking, the cow eats from a feeder. Milk flows through tubes to a tank. When the milking is done, the arm removes the milker. The cow leaves the stall.

milk tanks

milk tubes

ear tag ····▶

collar ····▶

Each cow has an ear tag for **identification**. They have collars that collect **data**. Collars send the data to a computer. The computer tells the farmer the weight of each cow. It records how much food a cow eats. It also shows how much milk comes from each cow.

DID YOU KNOW?

What if there is a problem with a robotic milker? Some machines can call the farmer on the phone. The farmer can use an app to fix the problem!

An AMS can milk about 175 cows each day! It allows the farmer more free time. It also saves money. How? Fewer people need to work to milk the cows.

Milkers help farmers. They are safe for cows. What more would you like to learn about them?

DID YOU KNOW?

Some farmers use robots to remove **waste** from the milking area. This saves time. It also helps keep everything clean.

ACTIVITIES & TOOLS

BY MACHINE OR BY HAND?

Machines can help us do tasks more efficiently. See how with this activity!

What You Need:

- dirty clothes
- laundry detergent
- sink or small tub
- clock or timer
- washing machine
- notebook
- pen or pencil

❶ Volunteer to help the next time laundry needs to be done. With an adult's help, use a small amount of laundry detergent to wash a dirty clothing item by hand in a sink or small tub. Set a timer when you begin. Record how long it takes.

❷ With an adult's help, load dirty clothes into a washing machine and run it with laundry detergent. Record how many items of clothing the washing machine is cleaning. Record how long it takes to load and start the machine.

❸ Compare your results. How long did it take to wash one item of clothing by hand? How long did it take the washing machine to wash multiple clothing items?

GLOSSARY

automatic milking system (AMS): A robotic system that replaces a person to do the job of milking cows.

bacteria: Microscopic, single-celled living things that exist everywhere and can either be useful or harmful.

calf: A young cow.

data: Information that is collected so something can be done with it.

efficient: Working very well and not wasting time or energy.

engines: Machines that make things move by using gasoline, steam, or another energy source.

herded: Moved together in a group.

identification: A document or other item that proves who someone or something is.

infections: Illnesses caused by bacteria or viruses.

robotic: Describing a machine that is programmed to perform complex tasks.

suction: The act of drawing air out of a space to create a vacuum. This causes the surrounding air or liquid to be sucked into the empty space.

vacuum: A sealed space or container from which all air or gas has been removed.

waste: What a body does not use or need after food has been digested.

INDEX

TO LEARN MORE

Finding more information is as easy as 1, 2, 3.

❶ Go to www.factsurfer.com

❷ Enter "milkers" into the search box.

❸ Choose your book to see a list of websites.

FACT SURFER